**Circulation: Please
check for disc in back.**

D1528578

PEOPLE WHO HELP IN MY NEIGHBORHOOD

By JANET PREUS

Illustrated by CHARLOTTE COOKE & DAN CRISP

CANTATA
LEARNING

MANKATO, MINNESOTA

WWW.CANTATALEARNING.COM

CANTATA
LEARNING
MANKATO, MINNESOTA

Published by Cantata Learning
1710 Roe Crest Drive
North Mankato, MN 56003
www.cantatalearning.com

Library of Congress Control Number: 2014957011
People Who Help in My Neighborhood
978-1-63290-270-2 (hardcover/CD)
978-1-63290-422-5 (paperback/CD)
978-1-63290-464-5 (paperback)

People Who Help in My Neighborhood by Janet Preus
Illustrated by Charlotte Cooke

Book design, Tim Palin Creative
Editorial direction, Flat Sole Studio
Executive musical production and direction, Elizabeth Draper
Music arranged and produced by Steven C Music

Printed in the United States of America.

VISIT
WWW.CANTATALEARNING.COM/ACCESS-OUR-MUSIC
TO SING ALONG TO THE SONG

In a **community**, people help each other. It takes many kinds of helpers to run a town. Who do you see helping in your neighborhood?

Now turn the page,
and sing along.

Letters in the mailbox—who put them there?

I know who it is. It's the mail carrier!

She sees your **address** on the letter and brings it to your door.

She'll deliver all the letters until there are no more.

People helping people, all around.

People helping people, in my town.

Where is the fire? The firefighters know.

Their red truck has a siren and a long water hose.

They help each other hook the hose up to a **hydrant spout**.

It takes a lot of water to put the fire out.

10

People helping people, all around
People helping people, in my town.

When **traffic** is a problem, police are on the spot.

In a black-and-white car with a light on the top.

Drivers can get a little crabby when they're moving slow.

But listen to her whistle, and she'll tell you when to go.

People helping people, all around
People helping people, in my town.

A garbage collector needs a great big truck.

And when it gets full, the **compactor** smashes it all up.

People helping people, all around

People helping people, sing it again!

People helping people, all around

People helping people, in my town!

SONG LYRICS
People Who Help in My Neighborhood

Letters in the mailbox—who put them there?
I know who it is. It's the mail carrier!

She sees your address on the letter and brings it to your door.
She'll deliver all the letters until there are no more.

People helping people, all around.
People helping people, in my town.

Where is the fire? The firefighters know.
Their red truck has a siren and a long water hose.
They help each other hook the hose up to a hydrant spout.
It takes a lot of water to put the fire out.

People helping people, all around.
People helping people, in my town.

When traffic is a problem, police are on the spot.
In a black-and-white car with a light on the top.

Drivers can get a little crabby when they're moving slow.
But listen to her whistle, and she'll tell you when to go.

People helping people, all around.
People helping people, in my town.

A garbage collector needs a great big truck.
And when it gets full, the compactor smashes it all up.

People helping people, all around
People helping people, sing it again!

People helping people, all around
People helping people, in my town!

People Who Help in My Neighborhood

Rock
Steven C Music

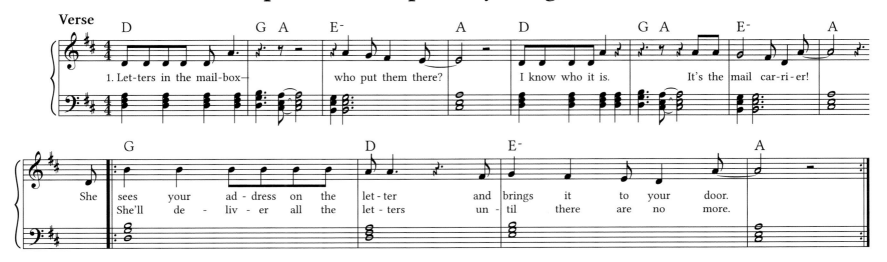

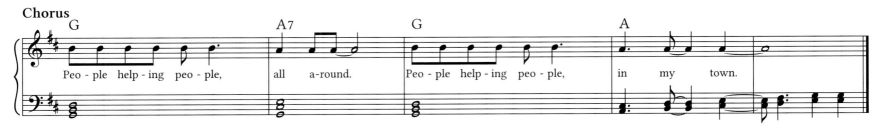

Verse 2
Where is the fire?
The firefighters know.
Their red truck has a siren
and a long water hose.

They help each other hook the hose
to a hydrant spout.
It takes a lot of water
to put the fire out.

Chorus

Verse 3
When traffic is a problem,
police are on the spot.
In a black-and-white car
with a light on the top.

Drivers can get a little crabby
when they're moving slow.
But listen to her whistle,
and she'll tell you when to go.

Chorus

Verse 4
A garbage collector
needs a great big truck
And when it gets full,
the compactor smashes it all up.

Chorus
People helping people, all around
People helping people, sing it again!

People helping people, all around
People helping people, in my town!

GLOSSARY

address—the writing on a piece of mail that shows where the mail is going

community—a group of people who live in the same area

compactor—a machine used to reduce the size of waste

hydrant—a large, upright pipe that draws water from the city's water supply; hydrants supply water for fighting fires.

spout—a tube or pipe that water flows out of

traffic—cars and trucks that are moving on a road

GUIDED READING ACTIVITIES

1. Who are the helpers in this book? What are their jobs?

2. Draw a map of your neighborhood. How is your neighborhood similar to the one in the book? How is it different?

3. What helpers have you seen in your neighborhood today?

TO LEARN MORE

Gregory, Helen. *A Firefighter's Day*. North Mankato, MN: Capstone Press, 2012.

Ready, Dee. *Police Officers Help*. North Mankato, MN: Capstone Press, 2014.

Rosario, Miguel T. A. *Mail Carrier's Job*. New York: Cavendish Square Publishing, 2015.

Zayarny, Jack. *Garbage Collector*. New York: AV2 by Weigl, 2015.